VLAD

A Life From Beginning to End

Copyright © 2016 by Hourly History Limited

All rights reserved.

Table of Contents

Vlad's early life and family

Rise to power: Vlad's first reign

War with the Ottomans, Vlad's main reign

Vlad's imprisonment, third reign, and death

Vlad Dracula's legacy

Vlad the Impaler in fiction: Count Dracula

Introduction

Movie lovers know the character well: a tall, dark, handsome man, dressed in a black cape, with a penetrating, seductive gaze. Women can't resist him and men can't best him. He is as alluring as he is lethal. He is Count Dracula, and he is world-renowned. Irish author Bram Stoker wrote the book *Dracula* in 1897, but where did Stoker get his inspiration? Is there any basis in fact to the story? Incredibly, in this case, the truth may, in fact, be stranger than fiction.

Stoker drew his inspiration, and the name Dracula, from Vlad III, Prince of Wallachia. Wallachia is a historical and geographical region of Romania situated to the north of the Danube River and south of the southern Carpathian mountain range[7]. Vlad III wrote his name as Wladislaus Dragwyla, but his Romanian patronymic is also written variously as Dragkwlya, Dagulea, Dragolea, and Drăculea. He was the son of Vlad II Dracul. Dracula, with the "a" on the end, is the diminutive form of Vlad's father's name. The name, Dracul, was given to Vlad II in 1431, the year of his infamous son's birth, upon his induction into the Order of the Dragon, a monarchical chivalric order established in 1408 by the King of Hungary, Sigismund, to protect Christianity in Eastern Europe. The word "drac" originally meant dragon, but in modern Romanian, it means devil[8,23].

Unlike his fictitious counterpart, who is often portrayed as tall and handsome, Vlad III Dracula was described as a short man who was stocky and strong. He was said to have a long, straight nose, a thin face, and green eyes with bushy, menacing eyebrows. He wore a mustache and had swollen temples that increased the bulk of his head. He also reportedly had a thick neck. His appearance, like his behavior, has also been described as cruel[8].

By most accounts, Vlad III Dracula, who was also known as Vlad Țepeș which in Romanian means "impaler," was born in Sighișoara, a Voivodeship of Transylvania in what was then the Kingdom of Hungary, but today is part of Romania. He was born in the winter of 1431 in either November or December; the exact date is unknown. His main reign as Prince of Wallachia lasted from 1456 to 1462, a period which coincided with the Ottoman wars in Europe, and more specifically, with the conquest of the Balkans. He had ruled in 1448 after his Turkish allies attempted to install him as Prince, but that coup was short-lived, lasting only two months. He would also rule again beginning in November of 1476, but that too would last just a little over a month, at the end of which he is presumed to have died[8,14,15].

It was during the war with the Ottomans (Turkish Muslims) that Vlad III paradoxically earned both a reputation for cruelty, which gave rise to the moniker Vlad the Impaler, and his revered status as a folk hero for his protection of Romania and Hungary. The moniker Vlad the Impaler was bestowed upon him posthumously around 1550, although he was previously known as Kaziklu Beg or Kazili Voyvoda, both of which mean

Impaler Lord. The name was so given by the Ottoman Empire after their soldiers came across what they described as "forests" of impaled victims. Impaling was his preferred method of execution. He is estimated to have killed somewhere between 40,000 and 100,000 people. He burned villages and fortresses to the ground and is said to have taken pleasure in torturing and killing his victims, even feasting amidst their remains. One German pamphlet written in 1521 describes how, among other grisly acts, he roasted children and fed them to their mothers. Such was his reputation in Western Europe. In eastern Europe, however, he fared much better[1,17].

Romanian and Bulgarian documents from 1481 onwards depict Vlad as a hero whose harsh but fair methods were justifiable, given that his motive was to reclaim his country. Additionally, his military efforts were all directed against the Ottoman Empire, which at the time was attempting to conquer Wallachia. Slavonic tales from the late 15th century and early 16th century describe him as hating evil in his country so much that he would kill anyone who attempted to harm it. Thus, he was seen as a folk hero in many areas of eastern Europe, though he was ultimately unsuccessful in repelling the Turkish invaders. The exact date and location of his death are not known, but he died at the age of 44-45 years old. He was buried by his rival, Basarab Laiota, without ceremony. The location of his burial is also not known, but it is possible it was at a monastery known as Comana, which was founded by Vlad in 1461[19,20]. Several subsequent searches for his burial have failed to yield results, and of course, at least one tale would have it that he never died at all, but goes on to torture his victims as one of the undead. It is easy to see how the mysterious circumstances that surround his death, along with his "taste" for blood, could give rise to such a tale.

Chapter One

Vlad's early life and family

"The Impaler, the Fallen Angel's son come."

—Hecatomb Tur, The Barbaric Deformity

Most accounts cite Transylvania, the central region of Romania, as Vlad III's birthplace, but at least one expert argues he may have been born in Târgoviște, which is located in the region of Wallachia. Florin Curta, a professor of medieval history and archaeology at the University of Florida, notes that Vlad III never owned anything in Transylvania, including the Bran Castle, which is often referred to as Dracula's castle and has been depicted in the fictional accounts as such. By all accounts, he never even set foot there. Vlad's father, however, did own a residence in Sighișoara, Transylvania, but Curta argues it is not certain that the Wallachian prince was born there. He notes that Târgoviște makes more sense as the site of Vlad's birth, given that it was the royal seat of the principality of Wallachia at the time of his birth, and it is where his father was a *voivode* or ruler [8,14,20].

Who Vlad's mother was is unknown. At the time of his birth, it is believed his father was married to Princess Cneajna of Moldavia, who was the eldest daughter of Alexander the Good, Prince of Moldavia. Vlad II, however, also kept a number of mistresses, and so it is possible one of them was Vlad III's mother. Vlad III had three siblings: two older half-brothers, Mircea II and Vlad Călugărul, and a younger brother, Radu III the Handsome. Vlad Călugărul's mother was one of Vlad II's mistresses, Caltuna, who later entered a monastery. Her son eventually followed in her footsteps and became Vlad the Monk. Vlad III Dracula would marry twice in his life and have at least three sons, one by his first wife whose name is unknown and who died in 1462, and two by his second wife, Ilona Szilágyi, a cousin of the King of Hungary. Some historians believe he also had a daughter named Maria with his second wife [8,11,14,20].

In the year of Vlad's birth, his father was inducted into the knightly order known as the Order of the Dragon. Upon his induction, he was given a new surname: Dracul, derived from drac, which, at the time, meant dragon. In modern Romanian it means devil. His son, therefore, was given the name for the son of Dracul, which in old Romanian is Drăculea. It is from this that the name Dracula is derived. The role of the Order of the Dragon was to protect Eastern Europe from the Ottoman invaders. It was established in 1408 by Sigismund, then King of Hungary, but who would later become Holy Roman Emperor (1433-1437). The order required its initiates to defend Christianity, particularly from the Ottoman Empire. It was modeled after the military orders of the Crusades, and it flourished during the first half of the 1400s. Sigismund died in 1437, and after that, the importance of the order declined in western Europe, though it continued to play a role in Hungary, Croatia,

Wallachia, and Serbia, locations which were, at that time, the target of Ottoman incursions [8,14,20,22].

Vlad and his younger brother Radu spent much of their early years in Sighișoara, but during his first reign, their father brought them back to the capital of Wallachia, Târgoviște. There, they would have been educated by Greek or Romanian scholars who were likely commissioned from Constantinople, the capital of the Byzantine Empire at the time. The skills they are believed to have learned include mathematics, geography, science, several languages including Old Church Slavonic, German, and Latin, the classical arts, philosophy, and of course, combat skills[2,8,14,20].

In 1436, Vlad II ascended to the throne of Wallachia and became Prince. He ruled until 1442 when he was ousted by rivals who were in league with Hungary. He negotiated Ottoman support to reinstate him by agreeing to pay tribute to the Sultan Mehmed II and leave two of his sons at the Ottoman court as a guarantee of his loyalty. The latter was not really a choice, but rather occurred when he took his two sons, Radu and Vlad Dracula, with him to meet with the Sultan. Once there, the boys were taken prisoner, though the time they would spend in captivity was considered privileged, and as a result, they were well-treated. In the Ottoman court, Vlad was educated in logic, the Quran, and the Turkish language, which he would come to speak fluently in his later years. Both he and his brother were also educated in horsemanship and warfare. Many believe that Vlad Dracula also spent some of this time in Constantinople in the court of Constantine XI Paleologus, the final emperor of the Byzantine Empire, which fell in 1453 to the Ottomans [8,14,20,22].

Unlike his brother Radu, Vlad resisted his captivity. Radu, on the other hand, acquiesced, and in fact, eventually converted to Islam and entered Ottoman service. Vlad, however, remained defiant, despite constantly being punished for his misbehavior. Some (Akeroyd 2008) have even suggested that the traumatic experiences he endured during his captivity may have shaped his sadistic nature later in life, particularly regarding his taste for impaling. While Vlad and his brother Radu were held at the Ottoman court, their father, Vlad Dracul, regained control over Wallachia, which had been wrested from his son, Mircea II, who had been ruling in his absence. Hungarian leaders were angry with Vlad II's alliance with the Ottomans, and subsequently, under the leadership of John Hunyadi, attacked Wallachia, forcing Mircea to flee and go into hiding. With the support of the Ottomans, Vlad II regained control over Wallachia[8,14,16,20].

In 1447, Hunyadi once again attacked Wallachia and was again victorious against the armies of Vlad Dracul and his son Mircea II. Vlad Dracul fled, but Mircea was captured, and subsequently blinded with a red-hot poker and buried alive. Vlad Dracul was also captured and killed a short time later. While Vlad the Monk was a contender for the throne, he took no active part in attempting to rule. That left Vlad III as the next in line[8,14,16,20].

Chapter Two

Rise to power: Vlad's first reign

"I am all in a sea of wonders. I doubt; I fear; I think strange things which I dare not confess to my own soul."

—Bram Stoker, *Dracula*

With both his father and older brother dead, and another older brother in a monastery, Vlad III was next in line to rule Wallachia. With Ottoman support, he was installed as leader in 1448, though his reign lasted a mere two months until his opponents, Hungarians who had taken control from his father and killed both his father and one of his older brothers, re-focused their efforts on Wallachia and were, yet again, able to regain control. After this, fearful of assassination, Vlad Dracula fled to Moldova, where he spent the next three years under the tutelage of his uncle, Prince Bogdan II, and his cousin Prince Stephen. The three became close friends, but when Prince Bogdan II was assassinated in 1451 by his brother Petru Aron, Vlad was once again forced to flee the ensuing turmoil along with his cousin Prince Stephen. They both reappeared in Transylvania, where they came under the mentorship of the Hungarian warrior John Hunyadi and the Hungarian King Ladislaus[8,14,16,20].

At the time Vlad Dracula re-emerged in Transylvania, Vladislav II was the ruler of Wallachia. There are conflicting accounts regarding how he came to the throne. Most sources say he assassinated Vlad II Dracul and was then put in power by John Hunyadi, the Hungarian leader who was vehemently opposed to the Ottoman Empire. Other accounts, however, say that Vladislav was helped by the Ottomans to replace Dan III, whom the Hungarians had put in power. Most sources, however, do not list a Dan III among the rulers of Wallachia, and Dan II was Vladislav II's father. Both Dan I and Dan II are listed among the rulers of Wallachia, but both ruled prior to Vlad Dracul's rule. It is possible that Dan III was Vladislav II's brother, but again, the records are ambiguous regarding his rule of Wallachia[8,14,16,20].

Whatever the truth may be about how he became the ruler of Wallachia, Vladislav II came into conflict with John Hunyadi when he did not assist in the Battle of Kosovo in 1448. As a result, Hunyadi took back some Transylvanian territory, and that prompted Vladislav to put a trade embargo in place against Brasov County, which was part of Hunyadi's Transylvania. Negotiations ensued, and it appeared the embargo would be lifted, but Vladislav then attacked a fortress in Făgăraș in an attempt to regain some of the territory. In the process, he burned some villages, and that led to Hunyadi's decision to send Vlad Dracula to depose Vladislav II. On August 20, 1456, Vlad III Dracula killed Vladislav II in hand-to-hand combat. Dracula was then once again installed as the ruler of Wallachia, thus beginning his second and main reign[8,14,20].

Chapter Three

War with the Ottomans, Vlad's main reign

"Desecrate the earth and father it with horror."

—Hollow, Vlad

Vlad III Dracula ruled Wallachia in accordance with his strict moral code, and any deviation was punished in accordance with his sadistic nature. To impale his victims, he would tie each leg to a horse and slowly force a stake through the body, often beginning in the orifices, such as the anus or vagina. He took care to ensure the stake was not too sharp so that it wouldn't cause a wound that was too rapidly fatal. Once the victim was sufficiently impaled, the stake would be lifted upright, and the victim would be further impaled by the weight of their own body as it slid down the stake. The victim would often take hours or even days to die, and their corpses would sometimes be left in place for months. While impaling was his preferred method of execution, he also is said to have boiled and roasted victims alive, cut off various body parts including limbs, noses, ears, and breasts, strangled victims, exposed them to wild animals, skinned them, and burned them alive. He is said to have arranged the bodies of his victims, particularly those he impaled, in geometric patterns, and he supposedly continued to practice his ritualistic killing on animals, such as mice and rats, when he was later imprisoned by the Ottomans[8,14,16,20].

On the domestic front, female chastity was of particular concern to him, and for women who had lost their virginity before marriage, those who strayed during their marriage, or who were unchaste as a widow, he doled out a particularly harsh penalty. They were impaled, often through the vagina, on a red-hot stake. He would also sometimes cut off their breasts, and it was said he forced their men to eat them. He also felt that beggars were living off the sweat of others, as it were, and that this was a form of thievery. According to legend, he invited them to a fabulous feast, and once they had eaten, he closed and locked the door to the dining hall, and proceeded to set it on fire. No one escaped the flames. In this way, he claimed to have eradicated poverty[8,14].

His military leadership, while equally cruel to his adversaries, was often surprisingly honorable. In 1457, one year after Vlad III Dracula regained the throne of Wallachia, he kept his word by helping his cousin, Prince Stephen, ascend Moldavia's throne. During the three years Dracula spent under his uncle Prince Bogdan II's tutelage, the three had become good friends and had promised that they would help each other when needed in the future. Dracula kept that promise by providing some 6,000 horsemen to assist Stephen in deposing Petru Aron, who had killed Bogdan II and forced Vlad and Stephen to flee Moldavia. Subsequently, Stephen's reign would become a long resistance against Ottoman incursions. New aggression against the Ottomans was instigated by Pope Pius II who, in September of 1459, pleaded for an end to internecine conflict in Europe to face what he referred to as Christianity's common enemy [8,14,16].

In January of 1460, Pope Pius II requested a new crusade against the Ottomans at the Congress of Mantua, a city in Italy where the council was held. His plan was for the crusade to last three years. The son of John Hunyadi, Matthias Corvinus, was to lead the effort, and for this, he received 40,000 gold coins to purchase ten Danube warships and gather an army of 12,000 men. The only European leader who showed any enthusiasm for the crusade was Vlad III Dracula, and in an effort to keep the Ottomans out of Wallachia, he allied himself with Corvinus[8,14,20].

Meanwhile, the Ottoman Empire, under Sultan Mehmed II, responded to the lack of European enthusiasm to the new crusade by going on the offensive, capturing the last independent Serbian city, Smederevo. Ottoman forces captured Hungarian general Mihály Szilágyi and tortured his men to death. The general himself, who had been Vlad III's only ally when he razed several Saxon villages in 1458 in response to a merchant revolt, was sawed in half. In 1461, the Sultan also convinced the despotic leader in Greece to surrender his stronghold, after which Corinth and the capital Mistra soon surrendered without struggle [3,8].

As for Wallachia, it had already been claimed by the Sultan as Ottoman territory, and as such, it was forced to pay tribute to prevent conflict. Later the same year of the

Congress of Mantua, the Sultan Mehmed II sent envoys to Wallachia to collect what was by then a late tribute amounting to 10,000 ducats and 500 recruits, called janissaries, into the Turkish armed forces. Vlad declined the envoys' request for payment, and on the pretext that they had failed to raise their hats to him - something they refused to do for religious reasons - he had their turbans nailed to their heads. Suffice it to say the Sultan was not pleased. The Turks began crossing the Danube and doing their own recruiting, to which Vlad III responded by having them impaled[3,8,14].

At the end of November in 1461, Vlad wrote the Sultan to say he couldn't afford to pay the tribute, but that he would send gold when he could afford it, and that he was willing to come to Constantinople to negotiate the payment if the Sultan would provide an interim leader in his absence. The Sultan, however, had received intelligence reports about Vlad's alliance with Corvinus, and he sent the bey (chieftain) of Nicopolis, Hamza Pasha, to ostensibly meet with Vlad, but his real agenda was to ambush him and bring him forcibly to Constantinople. Vlad learned of the plan and devised his own ambush in response. When Hamza Pasha and his cavalry, which consisted of 1,000 men, were traversing a narrow pass to the north of Giurgiu, Vlad and his forces attacked. The bey and his troops were soon surrounded and defeated. During the battle, Vlad's forces were among the first European crusaders to employ the use of gunpowder in what has been described as a "deadly artistic way." Almost all of the Turkish forces were killed, and most were impaled. Hamza Pasha himself was impaled on the highest stake, in deference to his rank[3,8,14,20].

Following the battle near Giurgiu, Vlad Dracula crossed the Danube River to attack regions in Bulgaria between Serbia and the Black Sea. Because he had become fluent in Turkish during his years of captivity in the Ottoman court, Vlad was able to disguise himself and infiltrate Ottoman fortresses. He ordered the guards to open the gates, and of course, when they did, he and his forces attacked. He went on to slaughter every enemy soldier he could find and any population that even sympathized with the Turks. His forces covered some 800 kilometers in approximately two weeks and killed over 23,000 Turks. In describing the attacks, Vlad wrote the following to his ally Corvinus in February of 1462[21]:

"I have killed peasant men and women, old and young, who lived at Oblucitza and Novoselo, where the Danube flows into the sea, up to Rahova, which is located near Chilia, from the lower Danube up to such places as Samovit and Ghighen. We killed 23,884 Turks without counting those whom we burned in homes or the Turks whose heads were cut by our soldiers… Thus, your highness, you must know that I have broken the peace."

The precise numbers of the dead were reported as the following[8,11,12,14,20]: At Durostor, 6,840, at Giugiu, 6,414, at Rahova, 1,460, at Eni Sala, 1,350, at Nicopolis and Ghighen, 1,138, at Hârsova, 840, at Turtucaia, 630, at Sistov, 410, at Turnu, Batin, and Novograd, 384, at Orsova, 343, and at Marotin, 210.

The Sultan Mehmed was, at the time, occupied in Corinth, and thus unable to attend to this himself. He sent his grand vizier, Mahmud, to destroy a port in Wallachia known as Brăila. Vlad Dracula engaged the 18,000 troops commanded by Mahmud and defeated the attackers. Reportedly, only 8,000 Turks survived. At this point, Vlad was celebrated for his success in the Saxon cities of Transylvania as well as in the Italian states, and even by the Pope himself. His victories and his growing reputation as the Impaler Lord frightened many of the Turks who, as a result, left the European part of the Ottoman Empire and moved to Anatolia. Upon hearing about these developments, the Sultan Mehmed decided to abandon his current conflict in order to attend to Vlad Dracula himself. Both men began their preparations for war[3,8].

Mehmed II prepared an army equal to what he had assembled when he sought to conquer Constantinople. He wrote to one of his grand viziers that he was taking 150,000 men into battle. Some historians have estimated the size of his army at 300,000 men. His forces consisted of Janissaries, which were elite troops, acings, which were archers, infantry soldiers, sipâhis, which were the feudal cavalry, saiales, which were slaves who, if they survived what were considered suicidal missions, would win their freedom, and azabs, which were pikemen. Additionally, there were beshlis who handled firearms, silahdârs, who protected the flanks and cared for the sultan's weapons, and the sultan's personal bodyguards. Among the Sultan's forces was Radu the Handsome, Vlad's younger brother. He commanded some 4,000 horsemen. In addition to the fighting units, the Turks also brought engineers and workers who would build bridges and roads as necessary, priests who would call the troops to prayer, astrologers to assist Mehmed in making his military decisions, and women who were to pleasure the men at night. The Ottomans also brought 120 cannons and their own fleet of ships consisting of 25 triremes, which were ships that had three rows of oarsmen as well as sails, and 150 smaller vessels. The army was transported by Danube shipowners, who were paid 300,000 gold pieces for doing so [3].

Vlad Țepeș, the Impaler Lord, wasn't able to amass nearly the force that the Sultan had assembled. He requested assistance from Corvinus but received none. As a result, aside from able-bodied men of military age, he also mobilized women and children 12-years-old and older, including Gypsy slave contingents. Sources estimate his forces at between 22,000 and 31,000, but consensus places the number at approximately 30,000. Additionally, his army was not as well-armed. They carried lances, swords, and daggers, and wore chainmail for protection, but they lacked the more advanced weaponry the Sultan had at his command[8].

Despite his smaller and less well-equipped army, Vlad Dracula was able to do surprisingly well against the Sultan's forces. He was able to kill some 300 janissaries shortly after the Sultan's forces disembarked at Vidin. He instituted a scorched early policy in response to the advance of Mehmed's army. He poisoned the waters and evacuated the population, including the animals, as the Turks advanced. He made so-called hit and run attacks against Mehmed's forces, and he waged a form of germ warfare by sending in people infected with deadly diseases, most notably bubonic plague, to mix with the Turks and infect them. The plague did, in fact, spread to the Sultan's army[3,8,12,14,15].

Despite their losses, the Sultan's troops continued to advance toward the capital city of Târgoviște, where Vlad's castle, the Poienari Castle built high above the Argeș River, was located. They had been unsuccessful in capturing the fortress at Bucharest or the island of Snagov, but nonetheless, they pressed on. According to an eyewitness account recorded by papal legate Niccolò Modrussa, who reportedly received the information from a Wallachian veteran, Vlad Dracula and his force of some 24,000 men had taken shelter in a mountain refuge near the capital city when the Ottomans arrived. When he realized he was left with two equally undesirable choices of either starvation or falling into his enemy's hands, he did something that even amazed the Sultan and caused him to praise his worthiness as a soldier and an adversary. Once again utilizing his fluency in the Turkish language, he reportedly disguised himself and entered the Turkish encampment. There, he learned the location of the Sultan's tent and that he had ordered his men to remain in their tents at night so as to avoid panic in the event of an attack. Vlad used this information to plot a stealth attack during the night, one in which he had planned on returning to the Sultan's tent and killing the Turkish leader[3,8,12,15].

Vlad divided his men to attack from two sides and used some of the Turks they had taken prisoner to penetrate the camp. Once inside the camp, they caused chaos throughout the night of June 17, 1462. They slaughtered, according to some sources, approximately 15,000 Ottomans while only losing approximately 5,000 of their own men. Vlad might have killed the Sultan himself were it not for the fact that he mistakenly went into the tent of two of the Sultan's grand viziers instead. His forces might also have done more damage if the other commander who was supposed to attack from the other side had not lost his nerve. At daybreak, Vlad broke off the attack and retreated to his mountain refuge. None of the Sultan's forces dared to follow. The source of the account said the Sultan was so despondent over the attack that he abandoned the camp and would have continued to flee were it not for some friends who forcibly brought him back[3,8,18].

Despite their low morale, the Sultan and his forces proceeded to advance into the capital city. They found it deserted, with the gates wide open. They also found the impaled army of Hamza Pasha, as well as Pasha himself, was impaled on the highest stake. The Sultan was said to have been so impressed by the sight of some 20,000 impaled soldiers that he remarked, "…a man who had done such things was worth much"[5]. Finding no more resistance, the Turks retreated on June 22, leaving Radu and his contingent of janissaries behind as the new ruler of Wallachia. Legend has it that after the Sultan's soldiers marched on the city of Târgoviște, Radu and his forces then proceeded to surround Vlad's castle, the Poenari Castle, located some 860 meters high on a cliff outside the city. Vlad's first wife, whose name is not known, was in the castle at the time, and upon seeing the army surround the castle, reportedly remarked she would rather feed the fish of the Argeș than fall into Turkish hands. She then, so the story goes, threw herself off the cliff into the river below[8].

While the Sultan's army proceeded to Brăila, where they burned the city down, and Radu the Handsome continued to make incursions into Wallachia, the remainder of Vlad's force had to rush to Chilia to defend the town after Stephen III of Moldavia, whom Dracula had helped ascend to the throne, attacked the town to regain control over it. After successfully defending the town and wounding Stephen III, Vlad retreated to Hungary, where he made battle plans with Matthias Corvinus. Believing he had Hungarian support, he made his way back to Wallachia in the fall of 1462. Corvinus, however, turned against the Impaler Lord and plotted an ambush for him at Castle King's Rock, located just inside the Wallachian state. Vlad was captured by Corvinus' own men and taken to Hungary, where he was imprisoned. Modern day scholars, like Corvinus' own contemporaries, don't know why he shifted his loyalties. Recent research suggests the possibility that he believed he could be named Holy Roman Emperor, and for that reason, he wanted to end hostilities with the Ottomans as soon as possible. This might have played a role in his decision to arrest Vlad, whom he accused of being in league with the

Turks, something he then claimed was justification for not protecting the area. By abandoning the area to the Turks, he effectively ended the anti-Ottoman crusades in eastern Europe, and that allowed him to focus on becoming Holy Roman Emperor as he fought the forces of the current Emperor, Frederick III, in Hungary. Corvinus would not defeat Frederick's forces, nor achieve the title of Holy Roman Emperor, but he was subsequently crowned King of Hungary in 1464[8,11,12,15].

Chapter Four

Vlad's imprisonment, third reign, and death

"Death must be so beautiful. To lie in the soft brown earth with the grasses waving above one's head and listen to silence. To have no yesterday and no tomorrow. To forget time, to forgive life, to be at peace."

—Oscar Wilde

After being captured by his former ally Matthias Corvinus, Vlad the Impaler Lord was initially imprisoned at the Oratea Fortress, which is located in what is today Podu Dâmboviței village. He later served time in Visegrád, near Buda. Evidence suggests he was imprisoned from 1462 to 1466, but the exact length of his term is debated. During his time in prison, he gradually regained favor with Matthias Corvinus. While imprisoned, he was able to meet Ilona Szilágyi, a cousin of King Matthias, and after Vlad converted to Catholicism, the two were allowed to marry. His release from prison occurred sometime around the time of his marriage, and scholars who doubt a prisoner would have been allowed to marry into the royal family suggest he was likely released before the marriage. The couple was given a house at Pest and would eventually have two sons, Vlad Tepelus and

Mircea. Vlad had another son from his first marriage, Mihnea the Bad. Mihnea would rule Wallachia from 1508-1509, but would be assassinated. Vlad Tepelus, also known as Vlad IV Dracula, would be an unsuccessful claimant to the Wallachian throne, and his younger brother, Mircea would fall ill and die in his mother's presence in 1482. Vlad also had an illegitimate son during this time, whom he named Radu. Three of his sons would have children of their own, at least one of whom, Alexandru II, would rule Wallachia (1574-1577). By all accounts, Alexandru, like Vlad, was also an extremely cruel ruler[8,11].

Despite the turn his life had taken, Vlad Dracula still had aspirations to regain the throne of Wallachia. He began preparations to do so with Stephen V Báthory, who had been a military commander, and was, at the time of his collaboration with Vlad, a Hungarian judge royal. He would later serve as voivode of Transylvania. The two planned to assemble a mixture of Transylvanian, Hungarian, Wallachian, and Moldavian forces to take the throne from Prince Basarab the Elder. Basarab had replaced Radu the Handsome, Vlad's younger brother, in 1473, although Radu twice returned to the throne after that. Radu, however, died suddenly in 1475, and Basarab was the ruler at the time Vlad III Dracula would seek to regain the throne. When Vlad's army arrived, Prince Basarab's army fled. Stephen Báthory placed Vlad on the throne and returned to Transylvania. This left Vlad with little support, however, and when he was confronted a short time later by a large Turkish army, he had fewer than 4,000 men with which to try to defend the throne. Needless to say, he was defeated, and this third reign, which he had declared on November 26, 1476, lasted only two months at best[8,11,18].

The circumstances that surround the death of Vlad III Dracula are unclear. There are several versions regarding how he died. Some say he was killed while fighting the Turks, but others say disloyal Wallachian boyars, who were aristocrats, killed him, also while fighting the Turks. Still others say he was killed on a hunt or on accident by one of his own men. A Turkish chronicler, Antonio Bonfini, says he was decapitated by the Turks and his head was sent to Constantinople, where it was preserved in honey and put on display as proof he was dead. The date of his death also remains a mystery, but it is evident he was dead by January 10, 1477[8,11,15].

The location of Vlad Dracula's body is yet another mystery. Some say he was buried unceremoniously by his rival Basarab the Elder in the Comana monastery, which Dracula had founded and built. The monastery was demolished in 1589 and rebuilt by Radu Serban, who was later a prince of Wallachia. Others claim he was buried at the Snagov monastery near Bucharest. The monastery had been used as a prison and torture chamber and had a trap door that would open when prisoners were praying before the Virgin Mary and drop them to their death onto sharp stakes. Archaeologists uncovered a casket covered with a purple shroud embroidered with gold at Snagov in 1931. The skeleton it contained was covered with fragments of faded silk brocade, which appears similar to an oil painting of Vlad Dracula. The casket also contained a cloisonné crown with turquoise stones and a ring, similar to what was worn by members of the Order of the Dragon, sewn into the sleeve. The contents of this burial were taken to the History Museum in Bucharest, but they subsequently disappeared, leaving no trace and adding to the mystique of Dracula. Still another researcher believes that Dracula was not, in fact, killed at this time. Rather, he was captured and held for ransom by the daughter he had with this second wife, Maria, who took him to Italy where he later passed away and was buried at the church of Santa Maria Nova. This claim, however, has been largely discredited given numerous misinterpretations of the find by the amateur historian and student archaeologist who investigated the burial and made the initial claim. Thus, the location of his body remains unknown to this day[8,14,15,16].

Chapter Five

Vlad Dracula's legacy

"Sometimes the world no longer needs a hero. Sometimes what it needs is a monster."

—*Dracula Untold*, Universal Pictures

There is no doubt that Vlad III Dracula made his mark on history. He was a harsh ruler and a cruel adversary, but it is also true that he was a gifted strategist. He was also, at times, an honorable ally. His legacy, like his life, is a mixture of tales from Romanian, German, and Russian sources. Many of these tales remain part of the modern Romanian folklore, though through time, they have become somewhat garbled and confused. Among the Romanian peasantry, pamphlets described Vlad Țepeș as a just ruler who protected and defended his people against foreign aggression. These sources also spoke of him as a champion of the common man because of his dislike for and resistance to aristocratic oppression. Despite his harsh tactics, Romanians also described him, in both their pamphlets and oral traditions, as an honest man who took great pains to eliminate crime and dishonesty. Even as late as 2004, a Romanian presidential candidate referenced Vlad and his methods of punishment for illegal activities as part of a speech against corruption[8,17].

Romanians also, however, described Dracula as an often capricious ruler who could be exceptionally cruel. Many of the alleged acts of cruelty, such as nailing their hats to the heads of the foreign ambassadors, are common to all of the pamphlets that describe him, whether of Romanian origin or elsewhere. Details sometimes vary, but the same basic story is found in all pamphlets regardless of their national origin. Some accounts describe his actions as justified, while others describe them as senseless acts of cruelty, and still others note that much of what he did was not unique to him, but rather common punishment at the time. Such was Vlad's reputation in Eastern Europe: a mixture of good and bad, honorable and cruel, justified and senseless. For example, in the Russian tales about Vlad Dracula, he is often depicted as a great and just ruler as well as a brave soldier. There are tales of atrocities, but those are frequently justified as the actions of a one-man ruler[17].

In western Europe, his legacy is much darker. He is viewed by most as a cruel madman, although the number of people he is alleged to have killed is likely exaggerated, and some argue that many of the specific acts of horror ascribed to Vlad are likely fictitious. The German stories are by far the darkest, in one case describing him as "…far worse than the most depraved emperors of Rome…"[8]. Many of these were written during Vlad's lifetime and with a political agenda. For example, Matthias Corvinus is believed to have played a role in blackening Vlad's image in order to justify his decision to end hostilities with the Ottomans and abandon the region of Wallachia to their rule. Despite the political motivations behind the stories, they soon became literature, and in fact, were best-sellers in the 15th and 16th centuries, thus widening Vlad's dark reputation. The invention of the printing press played a role in bringing these texts to a broader audience[17].

Vlad also left a different legacy: his descendants. He had at least three children by his two wives. One of his children, Mihnea the Bad, whom he had with his first wife, ruled Wallachia from 1508-1509. Neither of his other sons would ever gain the throne. After Vlad Dracula was killed, Mihnea ambitiously sought to rule. He utilized support from the boyars, the aristocracy, to organize a series of raids, but it wouldn't be until 1508 when he would successfully ascend to the throne and begin his rule, part of which he would share with his son, Mircea III Dracul, in 1509[8,16].

Like his father, he was devoted to Christianity and vehemently anti-Ottoman. He was dubbed "the bad" by his enemies, one of whom described him as a wolf in sheep's clothing, the latter of which he abandoned as soon as he became the ruler. He is said to have taken the boyars captive after ascending to the throne and to have treated them cruelly, often cutting off the noses and lips of some, and hanging and drowning others. He reportedly resorted to more of his father's tactics, though his assassination meant he did not have time to do the same amount of damage. Mihnea the Bad's son, Mircea III, continued to rule after his father's death, but in 1510, the throne was taken from him by Vlad cel Tânăr, who was the son of Vlad III Dracula's older brother Vlad the Monk[8,14].

Mircea III's son, Alexandru II Mircea, would also rule from 1568-1574 and again from 1574-1577. He, too, was known for his extreme cruelty. He is said to have slaughtered dissident boyars and was himself eventually poisoned by supposedly loyal noblemen. His son Mihnea Turcitul would take the throne after his father's death in 1577 and would rule until 1583. He would take the throne again in 1585 and rule until 1591. He is known as Turcitul because he converted to Islam; Turcitul means Islamized. In his last rule, he was deposed, and afterward, because he had converted, he was appointed as ruler of Nikopolis using the name Mehmed. His illegitimate son Radu Mihnea would take back the throne of Wallachia in 1601, the year that Mihnea Turcitul died in Istanbul. Thus, Vlad Dracula's legacy includes a long line of rulers, many of whom exhibited the same degree of cruelty as their infamous progenitor[8,11].

Chapter Six

Vlad the Impaler in fiction: Count Dracula

"The past is almost as much a work of the imagination as the future."

—Jessamyn West

Though Bram Stoker's *Dracula* is the most famous version of the vampire myth, it is by no means the first. By the time of Stoker's book, the vampire legend was deeply rooted in Eastern European folklore. Though there are legends of vampire-like creatures from all around the world, and many of these demons and spirits are considered precursors to the modern version, the vampire as it came to be known in Europe has its origins in southern Slavic and Greek folklore. Interestingly, although Stoker drew inspiration and the famous name from Vlad III Dracula, the vampire legend is absent in Romanian culture; there, of course, Vlad the Impaler is remembered as a hero[10,19].

    The vampire, as it was known in the Balkans, was an undead being, often bloated and with a ruddy or dark face, which wore shrouds and caused mischief and death in neighborhoods the person inhabited during life. The popular version known today of a gaunt, pale vampire didn't appear until the 19th century. In the original folklore, any corpse that an animal jumped over, particularly a dog or cat, could become one of the undead. Additionally, a body that had a wound which had not been treated with boiling water was susceptible to becoming a vampire. In Russian folklore, vampires were witches who had rebelled against the Russian Orthodox church[4,10,19].

Early vampire accounts in Medieval and European folklore appear in the chronicles of 12th-century English historians Walter Map and William of Newburgh, though the vampire proper did not appear until the 17th and 18th centuries. The first account of a real person being described as a vampire occurred in the region of Istria in modern Croatia in 1672. Jure Grando of the village Khring near Tinjan was reported to be a vampire who caused panic among the villagers. Jure had died in 1656, but the villagers claimed he returned from the dead to drink human blood and sexually harass his widow. The village leader ordered that he be staked through the heart, but that didn't kill him, and subsequently the leader gave the order that he be beheaded, which proved more effective[4,10,14].

During the 18th century, there was a flurry of reported vampire sightings in eastern Europe. This resulted in numerous and frequent stakings as well as grave exhumations to kill suspected vampires. Government officials were even involved in the activities, and the mass hysteria surrounding these beings spread throughout most of Europe. The first two officially recorded cases of vampirism involved two corpses in Serbia, one of Peter Blagojevich and the other of Arnold Paole. After returning from the dead, Blagojevich allegedly killed some of his neighbors, who died of blood loss. In the Paole case, people in the area surrounding where he lived began to die after his death, and he was believed to be the cause. In both cases, government officials examined the bodies, wrote case reports, and published books throughout Europe. The hysteria that resulted is referred to as the "18th-Century Vampire Controversy," and it raged on for a generation, probably aggravated by numerous accounts of vampirism in rural villages[4,10].

In response to the threat of vampirism, loved ones often took extraordinary precautions when burying the dead. They sometimes buried them face down, decapitated them, or placed scythes or sickles near their bodies to satisfy demons and/or prevent the dead from rising from their graves[4]. At the Medieval cemetery site of Kaldus, Poland, there were 14 "anti-vampire" burials uncovered. Some of these were decapitated while others were buried face down and still others were weighted down with stones. Experts believe that people sometimes mistook diseases that caused the victims to become pale or emit blood from various orifices as evidence of vampirism, but these skeletons showed no evidence of any such illnesses[13]. At another site in Poland, the Drawsko cemetery, which dates from the late 17th to early 18th centuries, four skeletons were discovered with sickles around their necks and a fifth skeleton had a sickle across its hips. While many interpret this as anti-vampire measures, the archaeologists who excavated the cemetery reject the term anti-vampire, and instead interpret the burials more broadly as anti-demon[9]. Still, the practice demonstrates evidence that the people of this region believed in the possibility that the dead could still be re-animated and pose a threat to the living.

Other methods used to prevent vampirism included practices such as severing the tendons at the knees, or placing poppy seeds, sand, or rice at the grave site to keep the vampire occupied; the belief being the vampire would be compelled to count the grains or seeds. Myths from Europe, China, India, and South America all contain similar themes associating vampirism with arithmomania, a type of obsessive-compulsive mental disorder in which victims feel compelled to count their actions or objects in their surroundings[4,10,14].

Identifying vampires also involved elaborate rituals, including leading a virgin boy through a graveyard on a virgin stallion. The theory was the horse would balk at a vampire's grave, but in accordance with most rituals, it must be a black horse. Holes appearing over the earth was another way to identify a vampire's grave. Other evidence of vampire activity included the deaths of animals in the area, and in some cases, poltergeist activity such as throwing stones or pressing on people during their sleep. Additionally, corpses that showed little or no decomposition were suspected of vampirism. In cases where graves of suspected vampires were opened, the villagers described them as having fresh blood on their face. Modern experts explain the presence of apparent blood as part of the normal process of decomposition. In modern times, vampires are mostly considered works of fiction and overactive imaginations, but there are some cultures where myths of blood-sucking creatures still exist. The chupacabra, or goat sucker, of Puerto Rico and Mexico, is but one example [4,10,14].

The association of vampirism with Vlad III Dracula wasn't made until Bram Stoker published his book in 1897, and even then, some scholars argue Stoker's Dracula was not based on Vlad the Impaler. The evidence that the two are connected is drawn from the fact that they share a name. Additionally, Stoker borrowed a library book by William Wilkinson entitled *An Account of Principalities of Wallachia and Moldavia,* published in 1820. The book contains references to Voivode Dracula and in a footnote mentions that Dracula means devil in the Wallachian language. Moreover, he extensively researched Balkan history and is sure to have learned about Vlad the Impaler. He also met with a friend of his, a Hungarian professor from Budapest named Arminius Vambery, who may have provided him with information about the historical Dracula. Furthermore, some of the text in Stoker's novel relates directly to Vlad III Dracula. For example, there is text which discusses fighting off the Turks, and the physical description of Dracula in the novel matches the image of Vlad the Impaler. Finally, there may be some correlation between the novel's treatment of the vampire myth and Vlad Dracula. Driving a stake through the heart of the vampire, for example, could be taken from Vlad's history of impaling his victims. Renfield's fixation with insects could be linked to the history of Vlad's imprisonment, where he was said to have tortured small animals. Additionally, Dracula's fear of holy objects could be correlated with Vlad's renunciation of the Orthodox Church[15,16].

Elizabeth Miller, a professor in the English Department at Memorial University of Newfoundland, argues there is no correlation between the historical Dracula and the work of fiction. She argues that Stoker doesn't mention Vlad III Dracula nor any of his atrocities in his notes, and as he was a meticulous note keeper, he would have done so if he was basing his character on the real Dracula. She also argues that the only thing Stoker may have learned from the library book that he borrowed was the name Dracula, and rather than the history of the person having caught his attention, it was simply the footnote where it states that the meaning of the word in Wallachian is devil. She argues that is why Stoker chose the name, especially since the book only discusses Voivode Dracula and how he crossed the Danube and attacked Turkish troops. It mentions nothing about his atrocities. She also argues that in meeting with his Hungarian friend, Professor Vambrey, there is no evidence the two ever spoke about Vlad Dracula, and she discounts the assertion that the likeness of the fictional Dracula was drawn from the real person. She believes it more likely Stoker used earlier villains in Gothic literature or other sources as inspiration for the appearance of his vampire[15].

Miller's arguments aside, many modern scholars do associate Stoker's Dracula with Vlad the Impaler, and the association has caught on in fictional accounts. There have literally been hundreds of books, movies, and television programs devoted to the subject of vampires, and many of those have adopted Vlad III Dracula as the model for the villain, often embellishing on the history of the Wallachian prince to suit their own story lines. Many have included the story of his wife plunging to her death, for example, as the main reason Dracula sought out vampirism. The association with vampirism and his portrayal in fictional accounts are most certainly not part of the legacy Vlad Țepeș would have envisioned, but in a strange twist of fate, he has been ensconced in literature as, ironically, an immortal being[16].

Conclusion

Vlad the Impaler lived his life during a particularly turbulent and violent episode in European history. Many rulers during this time used cruel methods to slaughter innocent civilians right alongside soldiers and committed what would be considered, by today's standards, as crimes against humanity. Was Vlad III Dracula any different? Were his methods any crueler than those of his contemporaries, or were they in line with what was considered normal for the period? Certainly, those who suffered by his hand would find his methods cruel and unusual, but to those he was protecting, he is a hero and a just leader [20].

While the truth surrounding the atrocities committed by Vlad the Impaler is a matter of some debate, it is certain that he was a skilled warrior and fearsome leader. He ruled Wallachia on three occasions, though two of those were very short-lived, and the last ended with his death. His main rule from 1456 to 1462 saw many victories, and even as he faced defeat from the advancing Turkish troops, his actions under pressure impressed even his enemies so much so that they complemented him a worthy adversary. He also honored his commitments to friends, something evident when he sent troops to assist his cousin, Prince Stephen of Moldavia, within a year of ascending to the throne in 1456. He had promised to help Stephen whenever and however he could during his three years of tutelage under his uncle Prince Bogdan II, and he kept his word [8,14].

He earned his feared reputation as the Impaler Lord during his main reign. In pursuing his goal of repelling the Ottoman Empire, he is said to have killed between 40,000 and 100,000 troops, mostly by impaling. In one battle alone, he is said to have impaled over 20,000 soldiers. His enemies described coming upon "forests" of impaled victims, and many were so frightened as a result that they left the Turkish region of Europe and returned to Anatolia [8,14].

Vlad could be equally as fearsome on the home front. While many considered him a hero for protecting them, the citizens he ruled also knew of his cruelties. He was particularly concerned with female chastity and would severely punish any woman found to be unchaste or adulterous. He was also particularly harsh on criminals, and he considered beggars to be committing a form of thievery. His punishments included impaling men and women by tying each leg to a horse and slowly advancing a sharp - though not too sharp - stake into one of the orifices, i.e. the vagina or anus, and up into the body. He didn't want the stake to be too sharp lest is cause too rapid a death. Once advanced far enough, the stake would be lifted upright, and the body would sink further down. The victims would often endure for hours or even days before dying, and staked bodies would be left in place for months at a time to deter others from making the same mistakes. Vlad Dracula was also known to cut off body parts of his victims, or skin them alive, or even boil them alive. He is said to have feasted among the bodies of his impaled victims and to have roasted children and fed them to their mothers. He is also said to have cut off the breasts of women and fed them to their men. Many of these actions, however, may have been normal for the times[8,14,20].

Vlad's brother was blinded by a hot poker and buried alive by his enemies. Another of Vlad's allies, General Mihály Szilágyi, was sawed in half by Turkish forces. Eastern Europe at this time was a violent place. Internecine conflict among warring factions often pitted family members against one another, and the Ottoman Empire was in the midst of attempting to conquer the region. Conflict was constant, with leaders often going from one war to another. That such conflicts led to these kinds of atrocities, however shocking, is not necessarily surprising. Vlad the Impaler, however, was notable for his cruelty even among his contemporaries, if not for the kind of atrocities he committed, then for the number of victims he tortured and killed. He became a legend in his own time; contemporary pamphlets provided details of his gruesome acts and terrorized his enemies. His legend lived on beyond his death as well [8,14,20].

Tales of Vlad the Impaler were told well after his death by Germans, Russians, and Romanians. Some referred to him as a just leader whose harsh methods were used rightfully to protect his people from hostile invaders. Others described him as worse than any other tyrants who had come before or after him. His atrocities became world renowned. Additionally, his legacy included numerous descendants. Vlad the Impaler had at least three children, some of whom had children of their own. Many of Vlad's descendants went on to be rulers of Wallachia. Several of them, such as Alexandru II, gained reputations, like their progenitor, as cruel leaders[8,11].

Finally, Vlad the Impaler Lord's reputation was revived in the modern world through his association with Bram Stoker's novel, *Dracula*. While some scholars dispute that Stoker drew his inspiration from the life and legacy of the Wallachian prince, there is strong evidence that he did. Stoker researched Balkan history, and it seems certain he would have learned of Vlad III Dracula. He certainly drew the name from a book that mentioned the fact that Dracula means devil in modern Romanian. Additionally, Stoker had a Hungarian friend who was a professor, and the two met on several occasions. It seems unlikely that they wouldn't have discussed Stoker's book and that those discussions wouldn't have led to talk of the history of the area, particularly once the name Dracula was mentioned[14,15,20].

Even if Stoker didn't draw his character from the life of Vlad the Impaler, modern works of fiction have certainly drawn the conclusion that he did, or at least, that Vlad III Dracula makes a good model for the character. Hundreds of fictitious interpretations of Dracula represent the character as the undead version of Vlad the Impaler, a man who chose to walk among the undead as a result of his wife's suicide in the face of the invading Ottoman Empire [8]. Added to the enigma that is Dracula is the mystery surrounding his death and the whereabouts of his burial. The date and manner of his death are unknown, as is the exact location of his final resting place. While there have been claims that his burial has been found, either the evidence has disappeared or been discredited[16]. In the end, it makes no difference. Vlad the Impaler has, in a sense, risen from the dead. His legacy lives on, and if the facts of his life are in any way accurate, his fictional namesake pales in comparison, pun intended, as a bringer of death.

References Cited

1. John Akeroyd, (2009). "The Historical Dracula: Monster or Machiavellian Prince?" *History Ireland* 17/2: p. 23.

2. *Angold, Michael (1997). The Byzantine Empire, 1025–1204: A Political History. London: Longman.*

3. Babinger, Franz (1978). *Mehmed the Conqeror – And his Time.* Princeton: Princeton University Press.

4. Barber, Paul (1988). *Vampires, Burial and Death: Folklore and Reality.* New York: Yale University Press.

5. Chalkokondyles 9.90; translated by Anthony Kaldellis, (2014). The Histories (Cambridge: Dumbarton Oaks Medieval Library), vol. 2 p. 393.

6. Coates, John F. (1989). "The trireme sails again." *Scientific American.* 261 (4): 68–75.

7. *eliznik. (n.d.) Romania's ethnographic regions - Wallachia (Țara Românească). eliznik.org.uk.*

8. Florescu, Radu R.; McNally, Raymond T. (1989). *Dracula, Prince of Many Faces: His Life and His Times.* Little, Brown and Company.

9. *Gannon, Megan, (2015). Sickle-Wearing Skeletons Reveal Ancient Fear of Demons. LiveScience.com.*

10. Garza, Thomas (2010). *The Vampire in Slavic Cultures.* United States: Cognella. pp. 145–146.

11. Giurescu, Constantin C. (2007). *The History of Romanians II.* București: BIC ALL. pp. 107–108

12. Dennis P. Hupchick, (1995). *Conflict and chaos in Eastern Europe,* Palgrave Macmillan, p. 58

13. Killgrove, Kristina, (2016) "Healthy 'Vampires' Emerge From Graves In Medieval Polish Cemetery." Forbes.com.

14. McNally, Raymond; Florescu, Radu (1994). *In Search of Dracula: The History of Dracula and Vampires* (Revised ed.). New York, New York: Houghton Mifflin Company.

15. Miller, Elizabeth (2005). "Vlad The Impaler." Vlad the Impaler. n.p.

16. *The Real Dracula: Vlad the Impaler. LiveScience.com.*

17. McNally, Raymond (1982). Origins of the Slavic Narratives about the Historical Dracula. In: Stephen Fischer-Galati & Radu R. Florescu & George R. Ursul (eds.) *Romania Between East and West. Historical Essays in Memory of Constantin C. Giurescu.* Boulder: East European Monographs, pp. 127–145.

18. Stanford Shaw, (1976). *History of the Ottoman Empire and Modern Turkey.* Cambridge: University Press, vol. 1 p. 13.

19. Townsend, Dorian Aleksandra, (2011). *From Upyr' to Vampire: The Slavic Vampire Myth in Russian Literature,* Ph.D. Dissertation, School of German and Russian Studies, Faculty of Arts & Social Sciences, University of New South Wales, May 2011.

20. *Treptow, K.W. (2000). Vlad III Dracula (the life and times of the historical Dracula). Center for Romanian Studies.*

21. Twiss, Miranda Twiss (2002). *The most evil men and women in history.* Barnes & Noble Books. p. 71.

22. Van Antwerp Fine, John (1994). The Late Medieval Balkans: A Critical Survey from the Late Twelfth Century to the Ottoman Conquest. University of Michigan Press.

23. Wilkinson, William. (1820). "Account of the Principalities of Wallachia and Moldavia: With Various Political Observations Relating to Them by William Wilkinson – Reviews, Discussion, Bookclubs, Lists." Goodreads.com.

Made in the USA
Columbia, SC
03 March 2019